W9-COJ-847

SPORTS GREAT
JIM
ABBOTT

—Sports Great Books—

SPORTS GREAT
JIM
ABBOTT

Jeff Savage

—Sports Great Books—

ENSLOW PUBLISHERS, INC.

Bloy St. & Ramsey Ave.   P.O. Box 38
Box 777   Aldershot
Hillside, N.J. 07205   Hants GU12 6BP
U.S.A.   U.K.

Library of Congress Cataloging-in-Publication Data

Savage, Jeff, 1961–
    Sports great Jim Abbott / Jeff Savage.
       p. cm. — (Sports great books)
    Summary: A biography of the one-handed pitcher of the California Angels baseball team.
    ISBN 0-89490-395-0
    1. Abbott, Jim, 1967– —Juvenile literature. 2. Baseball players—United
States—Biography—Juvenile literature. [1. Abbott, Jim, 1967– . 2. Baseball players. 3.
Physically handicapped.] I. Title. II. Series.
GV865.A26S28 1993
796.357'09—dc20
[B]

                                    92-522
                                      CIP
                                      AC

Printed in the United States of America

10 9 8 7 6 5 4 3 2

Photo Credits: Athletic Public Relations, University of Michigan, pp.15, 18, 23, 26, 31, 33,
37, 39; California Angels, pp.8, 12, 43, 45, 47, 51, 53, 56, 58.

Cover Photo: AP/Wide World Photos.

Contents

Chapter 1

Jim Abbott was born without a right hand. No one at Tiger Stadium in Detroit, however, seemed to notice as Abbott continued to throw pitches with his left hand past the Tiger hitters.

He had grown up in nearby Flint, Michigan, and his favorite baseball team was the Detroit Tigers. He liked their blue-and-white uniforms, and sometimes he would go to Tiger Stadium to watch them play.

Jim had always dreamed of being a major-league pitcher. Even with one hand, he knew he could achieve his goal. Now here he was pitching for the California Angels—against his favorite team.

His family and friends were very proud of him, and they came to Tiger Stadium that night to see him pitch. The game was broadcast on national television, and fans across the country were tuned in. The huge audience made him want to win even more.

When Jim walked out to the mound for the first inning, the

Jim never had a problem pitching with one hand.

crowd cheered. They admired him for never quitting, even though he had only one hand. He was their hero.

Jim was known for throwing a blazing fastball, and he was so excited to be pitching in Tiger Stadium that he threw even harder than normal this time. One by one, the Tiger batters grounded out or struck out and walked back to the dugout shaking their heads. By the fourth inning, the Tigers still didn't have a hit.

Detroit manager Sparky Anderson was very impressed with Abbott. In the fourth inning, he turned to his coaches and said, "Boys, that's no-hit stuff you're looking at."

The Angels scored a run in the second inning and then another run in the fifth inning to lead 2–0. Abbott retired three straight batters in the bottom of the fifth and then got three more batters out in the sixth inning to keep the no-hitter going.

The fans cheered as Abbott walked out to the mound in the seventh inning. They wanted the Tigers to win, but they also loved seeing their hometown hero pitching so well. The first batter grounded out to the shortstop. The next batter hit a fly ball to left field that was caught for the second out. Jim was just seven outs away from a no-hitter when powerful Cecil Fielder stepped into the batter's box.

Abbott whirled and threw to the plate, and Fielder hit a ground ball up the middle. Angels' shortstop Dick Schofield ran to his left and reached out, but the ball rolled just past his glove and into center field. The no-hitter was gone. The crowd stood and applauded in appreciation of Abbott. The next batter hit a high bouncer toward third base, and by the time the ball came down, he was safe, too. Abbott knew he was unlucky, but he had to concentrate on the next batter. He threw a fastball that the next batter barely touched with the end of his bat. But the ball squibbed along the ground and rolled through the infield for another hit.

Angels' manager Doug Rader came out to the mound and told Abbott that he had done well but he was finished for the night. Jim was disappointed as he walked off the mound. He had wanted to get a no-hitter. As he walked toward the dugout, he saw the crowd rise to its feet and give him a loud ovation.

Six Angels' relievers couldn't stop the hard-hitting Tigers, who eventually won the game, 4–3. Afterward, all the praise was for Abbott.

"He was throwing some mean stuff," said Fielder, who broke up the no-hitter.

Sparky Anderson was even more impressed, saying, "In another year or so, Abbott is going to be the premier guy in this league."

Sparky's words came true a little early. The Tigers arrived in California to play the Angels late in the season. The Tigers were still in the pennant race, and they really needed to beat the Angels. They found out they would have to bat against Abbott again. This time, the game was in Jim's home park.

The sun was beating down and the air was warm as Abbott stepped up on the mound, hoping for revenge. He had won four straight games, and people were beginning to talk about him as a candidate for the Cy Young Award (the Cy Young Award goes to the best pitcher in the American League and to the best pitcher in the National League). Abbott laughed at the idea that he would be considered for such an important award. He wasn't concerned with winning the award, only with beating the Tigers.

Abbott gave up a hit early in the game, and the pressure of pitching a no-hitter was quickly off. Once again, though, Jim confused the Tiger batters. Inning after inning, the players from Detroit swung and missed at Jim's rocket fastball and hard slider.

In the sixth inning, Jim brought the crowd to its feet with a great fielding play. Jim couldn't hold the glove because he didn't have a right hand, so he cradled the glove in his right arm and switched the glove to his left hand after every pitch, in case the ball was hit back to him. With a runner on first, the batter hit a hard one-hopper at Abbott. By the time the ball arrived, Abbott had transferred his glove to his left hand. He fielded the ball with his glove, then quickly took off the glove and grabbed the ball out with his left hand. He spun around and threw to second base. Out. The throw was in time to get the runner.

The great play by Abbott inspired the rest of the Angels. In the bottom of the sixth inning, the Angels scored a run.

Since joining the Angels in 1989, Jim has been a bright star.

This time, Abbott would not let the lead escape. He continued to baffle the hitters until he was replaced in the eighth inning by a relief pitcher. The Angels held on to win 1–0, and Abbott had his fifth straight victory of the year and the first over the Tigers.

Newspaper reporters and camera crews gathered around Abbott in the Angels' locker room after game. They asked him how he felt about beating his old hometown team. Abbott was very humble, as usual, but also very proud.

"Beating Detroit and their lineup says something because they're in the middle of a pennant race," Abbott said. "I'm sure I'll be getting a few phone calls from people I know about beating them."

Abbott admitted he still was a Tigers' fan. "I'll be rooting for the Tigers the rest of the way," he said. "It's fun watching them in the pennant race."

The Tigers went on a tough losing streak and eventually finished behind the Blue Jays in the standings. Tigers' manager Sparky Anderson said after the season that the loss to Abbott in California was the game that most hurt the Tigers' chances.

The Angels had a poor season, but Abbott was a bright star, eventually winning 18 games and losing only 11 with a spectacular earned-run average of 2.89. Jim finished third in the voting for the Cy Young Award. He was surprised but, once again, very proud. It was another great accomplishment for Jim, who by now had a closet full of trophies and awards.

Chapter 2

Jim Abbott was five years old when he came running into the house and burst into tears. His mother, Kathy, and father, Mike, were in the living room. Jim ran up to his parents—crying.

"The other kids," he said, "won't let me play with them."

They had chosen up sides to play a game, and he didn't get picked. Kathy and Mike wanted to take Jim into their arms and tell him that everything would be all right.

"We wanted to hug him," his father said. "But we knew the best thing to do was to send him right back out there."

Mike and Kathy turned Jim around and sent him back outside.

"Now, you go tell them you want to play," Jim's father told him.

Jim walked slowly back out the door.

It was hard for him to grow up without a right hand. His arm went past his elbow and all the way down to his wrist. But he didn't have any fingers. The other kids were frightened at how it looked. Sometimes, they were very cruel and teased him. They would tell him it looked like a foot. It wasn't a nice thing to do, and it only made Jim feel worse.

When Jim was six, his parents took him to see a doctor. The doctor put an artificial hand on Jim called a prosthesis. The hand was made of fiberglass, and it had a metal hook on the end of it. It looked very scary.

With his new artificial hand, Jim could pick up objects, and he could tie his shoelaces and cut paper with a pair of scissors. He could do a lot of new things that he could never do before. The other kids were afraid of the metal hook, though, especially when Jim would swing his arm around with it. They thought it was creepy, and sometimes they would make fun of Jim. He hated the prosthesis and told his parents he didn't want to wear it anymore. They let him quit wearing it after six months.

People often told his parents that Jim should be put in a special school. After all, they said, he had a disability and would need special attention. Jim didn't like the idea. He told his parents that he wanted to be treated like all the other kids. Jim's parents understood.

Jim loved sports. He played basketball and football and especially liked playing soccer because he was really good at using his feet. His favorite sport, however, was baseball. Jim would sometimes spend hours throwing a ball against a wall near his house. All the time, he would pretend he was pitching to major-league batters. He would wind up and throw tricky curveballs that would fool the imaginary batters. Then he would rear back and throw fastballs right past them. He dreamed of one day being a major-league pitcher. All the kids in Flint where Jim grew up played baseball, and Jim liked playing with them.

Two of Jim's boyhood friends, Mark Conover and Howard Croft, went everywhere with Jim. During the

Jim always felt comfortable in a baseball uniform.

summer, they would go to the park or go fishing or just sit around and talk. More than anything, they played baseball.

Jim and his friends often would use a whiffle ball. They would set up a lawn chair on Jim's front lawn as a backstop behind the batter. They would draw lines for a single, a double, a triple, and a home run, and the batter would try to hit the ball past the lines. Jim and his friends would play until it was time for supper or until it got dark.

Jim's father would sometimes stick his head out the front door and holler, "Hey, you kids. You're tearing up the front yard. Go play somewhere else."

Jim would ask his dad if he and his friends could play just a little longer and his dad would say, "Well, OK," and then close the door. Jim's father and mother just wanted their son to be happy. They often told him to "dream of anything."

By playing so much whiffle ball, Jim became a good enough player to try out for a Little League team. When Jim arrived at the field the first day, the coach asked him what position he wanted to play. Jim didn't hesitate. "Pitcher," he said.

The coach said he would let Jim try playing pitcher but that Jim would have to prove himself. Jim did just that. In his first game with the midget-league team, Jim pitched five innings and didn't allow any runs or hits. He was a natural.

Jim continued to pitch in Little League, and when he was twelve, his hometown newspaper, the *Flint Journal*, wrote a story about him. When Jim was asked who his favorite major-league baseball player was, he said he liked them all.

"I look at them and wish it was me," Jim said.

By the time Jim got to high school, he had developed what everyone called "That Great Abbott Switch." Jim and his father figured out a way for Jim to pitch, field with his glove, and throw a runner out—all with his left hand. How? Jim would hold the glove between his right arm and his chest until he threw the pitch. Then he would slip the glove on with his left hand, in case the ball was hit back to him. Then after fielding the ball, he would pull the glove off with his right arm, reach in with his left hand and grab the ball. He could then throw out the runner.

Opposing teams tested him right away. In Jim's first game pitching for Flint Central High School, the first batter tried to bunt on him. Jim ran off the mound, fielded the ball, and threw the runner out at first base. Jim smiled to his teammates. He knew the hard work of learning to switch his glove was going to pay off.

Opposing teams weren't convinced. In another game in his freshman year, a team had its first eight batters try to reach base by bunting on him. The first batter reached safely. Jim threw out the next seven.

Jim compiled a 6–4 record his sophomore year, and colleges were beginning to notice. By the time Jim was a junior, coaches and scouts from different colleges began showing up at his games to see him pitch. He won 8 of 11 games as a junior and made Flint's all-city team for the second year in a row.

Jim had such a strong left arm that he also played quarterback for the school football team. He was mostly a backup his junior year, but he started several games his senior year, including an important playoff game against rival Midland High.

Midland had a good offense, so Jim and his teammates knew they would have to score a lot of points. They told Jim to pass, and he did everything he could, throwing four touchdown passes. It was enough to beat Midland, 26–20.

"The kid is talented, but the thing he's really got is guts," head coach Jim Eufinger said after the game.

Jim's parents often told him to "dream of anything."

Jim was eager for the baseball season to start. He wanted to go to college, and he wanted to have a good senior year so he could go to a good university. His teammates made him one of the team captains.

Jim was virtually unhittable in his senior year. His fastball sometimes went almost 90 miles per hour, and hitters didn't stand a chance. Jim finished the season 10–3 and had four no-hitters. At the plate, Jim gripped the bat and his right wrist with his left hand. He hit a remarkable .427 with seven home runs to lead the team.

Several colleges asked Jim to come to their school, and Jim chose the University of Michigan. Jim always liked the Michigan football team, and he knew the baseball team was good, too. He also liked Michigan because it was close enough to his home so his family could watch him play.

Everyone at Flint Central marveled at Jim's athletic ability, but they knew Jim had more going for him than that. Jim was one of the hardest workers on the team and in the classroom, and he always paid attention to his coaches and teachers. Some people wondered if Jim would be good enough to pitch against the collegiate players. Jim's friends and teachers at Central had no doubts. They knew what he could do if he kept up the hard work.

Chapter 3

As Jim Abbott walked toward the field in his new Michigan uniform, he noticed the NBC television cameras. The Wolverines were about to play their season opener against Villanova in a tournament in Orlando, Florida. Jim knew the game was important and that he would be the pitcher for Michigan, but he wondered why a national TV network was there. He already was nervous enough. He soon discovered that the cameras would be filming him. Jim always knew that he was special because he had no right hand, but now he was embarrassed. He just wanted to be recognized as a pitcher.

Jim tried to concentrate on the game. It was his first college game, and he wanted to impress his coaches and teammates. How much better, he wondered, were college hitters compared with high school players. When Jim stepped up on the mound in the first inning, he saw the cameras aimed right at him. He got very nervous. He took a deep breath and blew it out. Then he looked in for the sign from the catcher. He reared back and threw a fastball right down the middle of the plate.

"Steee-rike!" the umpire shouted. Jim felt relieved. Just then, the coach from Villanova came running out of his dugout toward the home plate umpire. "How could you call that a strike?" the coach shouted. The Villanova coach complained that the umpire was unfairly rooting for Abbott because he was special. The coach and umpire argued for several minutes. Jim stood on the mound, getting more upset and nervous as he waited.

"Jim was rattled after that," said Michigan sports information director Jim Schneider, who was at the game. "He just collapsed because there was so much pressure on him."

Jim got out of a bases-loaded jam in the first inning but gave up three singles and a walk in the second inning and was taken out of the game. The NBC camera crews left. Michigan won the game, 8–4, but Jim was disappointed with his Michigan debut.

Four days later, the Wolverines played North Carolina, and it was Jim's turn again to pitch. This time the game was in Winter Park, Florida. As Jim was putting on his Michigan uniform, he heard that the NBC cameras were there again to film him. He tried not to get nervous this time, but by the time he got to the mound, he was scared. This sure wasn't anything like pitching back in Flint, he thought.

Jim was so nervous that he walked the first three batters. He looked around the infield and saw that the bases were full, and at that point he got angry with himself. He knew he was better than that. He decided it was time to forget about the pressure and the cameras and just pitch as hard as he could. He got the next batter to ground into a double play, and then he picked a runner off first base to end the inning. That was more like it, he thought.

In the second inning, Jim calmed down. He struck out the first batter he faced. Then he walked a batter. North Carolina's

Pitching for the University of Michigan was a big challenge.

strongest hitter was up next. Jim threw him a fastball, and the North Carolina hitter smashed it deep over the fence for a home run. Jim got so upset that he walked three more batters and was removed from the game. Again, the NBC camera crew left. Michigan went on to win, 17–8, but Jim was mad at himself for pitching so poorly for the second game in a row.

Jim had always been encouraged to try as hard as he could, and everyone told him that he could do anything he wanted. But cynics would whisper that not having two hands might eventually stop him from getting to his ultimate dream—to be a major-league pitcher. Could they be right? Jim wondered.

The Michigan coach decided to take the pressure off Jim by letting him pitch in relief. He put Jim in a game a few days later that Michigan was losing by a run to North Carolina. It was the seventh inning, and there were runners at first and third. Jim threw a couple of pitches to the first batter he faced, and then the North Carolina coach decided to test Jim's fielding ability. He signaled for the runner at third base to try to steal home. Jim threw the next pitch to the plate. The catcher caught it and lobbed it back to Jim. Right then, the runner at third took off and dashed for home. Jim switched the glove to his left hand and caught the ball, pulled his fingers out of the glove, reached in the webbing, grabbed the ball, and fired it home. It was in plenty of time to get the runner who was out by 30 feet. Inspired by his fielding play, Abbott's Michigan teammates scored two runs in the seventh inning and two more in the eighth to win, 6–3. Jim had won his first college game.

The Wolverines returned to Ann Arbor, Michigan, a few days later, and it was announced in the campus newspaper that Jim would be pitching in the team's home opener. That day, a large crowd gathered at Michigan's Ray Fisher Stadium to see the freshman that everybody was talking about. The fans at Michigan were used to seeing good baseball players like Chris Sabo and Barry Larkin, and they wondered if Jim would fit in.

Jim showed everyone just how good he was. The game was against Grand Valley State University, and Jim was confident from the start. He remembered how nervous he had been down in Florida and told himself not to let it happen this time. The first batter popped up in foul territory, and Abbott came running over to make the catch. The crowd was amazed at Jim's defensive skills. Jim got the next two batters out as well.

The first batter in the second inning hit a sharp grounder up the middle. Jim reached out and snared it with his glove, turned, and threw to first for the out. Now the crowd was buzzing. In the third, a batter hit a ground ball between first and second base. The second baseman fielded the ball, but the first baseman was nowhere near the bag. Jim sprinted over and caught the throw just in time to get the out. The Michigan fans realized that Jim was not only a good pitcher but also a gifted fielder. He didn't allow any hits in the fourth inning, either, and the coach decided to replace him at that point. Scott Kamieniecki, now a pitcher for the New York Yankees, came in to pitch the rest of the game, and he didn't allow any hits either. Jim and Scott had combined on a no-hitter in the school's home opener.

Word of Abbott's ability began to spread across the country, and when he beat Western Michigan 1–0 later in the season, the ESPN sports network honored him as the Amateur Athlete of the Week.

Abbott would finish with a 6–2 record his freshman year. In the Big Ten tournament championship game that year, Michigan was trailing Minnesota 4–3 in the third inning when

Nobody worked harder in practice than Jim Abbott.

Jim came in to pitch. He didn't allow a hit until the eighth inning, and the Wolverines rallied to win, 9–5.

Jim's sophomore year was even better. He posted an 11–3 record, had an earned-run average of 2.08, and at one point didn't allow an earned run for 35 straight innings. After the season, Jim's teammates and coaches suggested that he try out for the United States national team during the summer. Team USA, as it is called, plays against teams of other countries, and that summer it would be competing in the Pan Am Games.

Jim tried out for Team USA in Millington, Tennessee, and he made the team as a starting pitcher. He would still pitch for Michigan during the college season, but for the next two months he would represent the United States as a member of its national team. It was Jim's biggest challenge so far, but he had made it this far, and there was no reason why he couldn't keep going.

Chapter 4

The newspaper reporters and television cameras seemed to follow Jim Abbott wherever he went. Now that he was on the United States national team, everybody wanted to know about him. He was becoming a bigger success story than he ever imagined. Though he always hoped to become a major-league pitcher, he never dreamed he would receive so much attention along the way.

The main question everyone wanted to know was, "What's it like playing baseball with just one hand?" He was asked the question over and over again, and he always took the time to answer it. Jim was learning a lot about patience.

"I just go out and play," Jim said. "I don't think about having one hand. I never do. I never have. I'm thinking about throwing the ball inside to a hitter who's weak on the inside pitch. I'm thinking about throwing a curveball. I'm not thinking about proving that I can play with one hand."

Jim didn't let all the attention about his disability distract him from pitching well for Team USA. During the summer tour to different countries, Jim won eight games and had an earned-run average of 1.70. He was named the starting pitcher in the most important game of the tour—against Cuba in Havana, Cuba. No team from the United States had beaten mighty Cuba in Havana in twenty-five years. Jim became the first. He confused the Cuban hitters all day with his hard slider, and the Americans won, 8–3.

His 8–1 record was the best on Team USA, and he was such an inspiration that he was chosen to lead all the American athletes in the opening ceremonies of the Pan Am Games at the Indianapolis Motor Speedway. Jim carried the flag, and thousands of fans cheered and waved American flags from the stands as Jim led the athletes across the field.

"I've never run across a feeling on a baseball field quite like that," Jim told reporters. "When you're out there, and the national anthem's playing, and you're holding your hat to your heart, it feels great."

Jim faced the team from Nicaragua in the first game, and he was brilliant from the start. The first batter tried to bunt, but Jim fielded it cleanly and threw the runner out. He pitched five innings and allowed only three hits as Team USA won, 18–0.

Jim didn't allow any runs in his next game, either, as Team USA won again. His last performance in the Pan Am Games, in the semifinals against Canada, would be his biggest challenge. Jim knew his team wouldn't score very many runs against the tough pitchers from Canada, so he figured he had to keep the game close by shutting down the Canadians. Jim held Canada scoreless, and Team USA managed to score twice to win, 2–0.

Later, he was named the winner of the Golden Spikes Award, which is presented to the outstanding amateur baseball player in the country by the United States Baseball Federation.

Among his many awards, Jim was named the most
outstanding amateur baseball player in the country.

Jim couldn't believe it. They were saying he was the best baseball player in the country who wasn't on a pro team.

The awards kept coming. By winning the Golden Spikes Award, Jim was nominated for the prestigious Sullivan Award, which goes to the best amateur athlete of the country in any sport.

The Sullivan Award had never been given to a baseball player in the fifty-eight years that the award had been in existence, but Jim felt that just to be nominated for it was an achievement. He was at Michigan when he found out he would have to go to Indianapolis for the award ceremony. He was scheduled to give a speech in his communications class the next day, so he called his professor and told her that he had to leave town for a few days. The teacher asked if it had something to do with baseball and Jim told her it did. She told him to be sure to bring her a note from his baseball coach to get excused from the class.

Jim sat up on the stage in his suit in Indianapolis and looked around. He couldn't believe he was sitting with all the great athletes from other sports. There was the basketball player David Robinson and the diver Greg Louganis and the swimmer Janet Evans and the volleyball player Karch Kiraly and the track star Jackie Joyner-Kersee all sitting right there with him. There were over 1,000 people in the audience, sitting at tables eating dinner. They were all dressed up.

When they announced the winner, Jim nearly fell out of his chair. It was he. The winner of the Sullivan Award was Jim Abbott. He couldn't believe his ears. "You picked the worst athlete up here," he said. At first he was embarrassed. Then he was overcome with pride.

He stepped up to the microphone to make a speech. "I would like to think that pure athletic ability was the reason I won," Jim said, "although I know the other thing [his

Jim won twenty-six games in a brilliant career at Michigan.

handicap] had a lot to do with it. But I think that's good, too. If this helps other people out somewhere else in the United States to move out and do things, then I'll accept it and keep going on."

Jim thought about his teacher who wanted him to bring a note from the coach. "I'll bring the trophy, instead," he said.

When Jim's junior season at Michigan began, he had trouble concentrating. So much had happened to him so quickly. He had been to so many places and won so many games and awards that pitching for the Wolverines just didn't seem the same anymore. He had a good year, winning nine games, including back-to-back shutouts over Purdue and Adrian. Still, he felt that it might be time to move on.

After Jim's junior year, he announced that he was going to turn pro. Thus he became eligible for the baseball draft in June. The California Angels selected him with their first pick, the number eight pick overall. Jim was happy. The Angels were a popular team, and they played their games in sunny Southern California. He figured he would pitch a year or two in the minor leagues before making the big-league team, but that was fine. His dream of being a major-league pitcher was getting closer all the time.

Before Jim joined the Angels farm system, he played one final summer on Team USA. It was an important summer. The team would be competing in the Olympics in Seoul, South Korea. Jim was named a starting pitcher on the team. He was about to get one more big thrill before becoming an Angel.

Chapter 5

Jim could hardly stand still in his Team USA uniform as he waited with his teammates and the rest of the American athletes outside the stadium in Seoul, South Korea. Jim had won so many big games and awards that his head was spinning. He knew that in a few months he would be a member of the California Angels. There wasn't much more that he could ask for or imagine. Nothing could top this moment, though. Jim was about to be in the 1988 Olympics.

Jim looked around and recognized faces that he had seen on television. There was track star Carl Lewis and tennis player Chris Evert and many others. Chris was running around with her camera taking pictures of all the athletes. She even took a picture of Jim. Everyone was waiting to march in the parade for the opening ceremonies. Jim couldn't believe he was here.

"It's almost weird," Jim told reporters. "It seems like the ideal plan I had coming out of high school worked. Everything just fell my way. I had great people behind me.

My coach at Michigan taught me how to pitch. I grew and got stronger. And here I am in the Olympics."

At the Olympics, everyone became fascinated with Jim. People who hadn't seen him before were amazed that he could play baseball with one hand. Foreign athletes and reporters came up to meet him. Six different television camera crews from Japan followed him around. Jim was one of the most talked about athletes at the games.

One day, Jim and some of his teammates went to Itaewon, the big shopping district in Seoul. Jim was surprised at all of the strange things that were for sale. This certainly was a different country than the United States, he thought. Jim spotted a football for sale among all the merchandise. He bought the football for $8. He saw tennis star Gabriela Sabatini and introduced himself. She already knew who he was. Jim had a friend take a picture of them together.

"Every day in the village, you go to eat and you see Matt Biondi or Steffi Graf or somebody," Jim said to the reporters. "It seems like every day, a new memorable event takes place."

Meanwhile, on the baseball field, Abbott's team was winning its share of games. Team USA was sailing through the competition, on its way to the playoff bracket round. Jim pitched in a few games and impressed everyone with how hard he threw. He gave up four hits in the three games but didn't allow a run in any of them. Eventually, the Americans reached the gold medal game against powerful Japan. American Olympic coach Mark Marquess was so impressed with Abbott that he named him the starting pitcher for the gold medal game. "As a person, they told me Abbott was the All-American boy—almost too good to be true," Marquess said. "But he's surprised me. He's almost better than that, if a person can be. As a pitcher, I expected him to be a polished left-hander. What I didn't know is that, right now, he's the hardest thrower on my staff."

The coach said Abbott could throw fast enough to keep the hard-swinging Japanese hitters on their toes. Japan was so good that in the 1984 Olympics in Los Angeles, they beat the United States in the gold medal game, even though Team USA had stars like Will Clark, Mark McGwire, and Barry Larkin. Jim knew he had a tough job ahead.

The fans packed Chamshil Baseball Stadium on the day of the game. Jim was going against Takehiro Ishii, the ace of Japan's staff. Japan scored first in the second inning to take a 1–0 lead. In the fourth inning, the United States took the lead when Tino Martinez hammered a two-run homer over the center field fence. Team USA added another run in the fourth and then another in the fifth to take a 4–1 lead.

By the age of twenty, Jim's fastball blazed at almost ninety miles an hour.

Abbott was sailing along, confusing Japan's hitters by mixing a hard slider with his blazing fastball. A small group of American fans in the stands waved mini American flags in support of Jim.

In the sixth, Abbott ran into trouble. He gave up two hits and a walk to load the bases, and then he walked another batter to force in a run. A ground ball forced in another run, and suddenly the score was 4–3. The coach was just about to take Abbott out of the game, but he changed his mind at the last moment. Jim managed to escape the inning with Team USA clinging to a one-run lead.

Jim settled down and began throwing strike after strike. He got the Japanese hitters out in order in the seventh inning and again in the eighth inning. Now he was just three outs away from winning the gold medal for his team. In the bottom of the eighth, Martinez, the hitting star, smashed another home run to make it 5–3.

Jim just needed to get through the ninth inning to win the game. The first batter grounded out to third base. So did the second batter. Now Jim was just one out away from the victory. He took a deep breath and threw to the plate. It was another grounder to third. The throw sailed over Jim's head on its way to first base—in time for the final out.

Jim leaped high in the air with his arms raised. He ran over toward first base to hug Martinez. The rest of Jim's teammates raced over and piled on top of him. Jim was at the bottom of the dogpile, but he didn't care. He was thrilled to win the game for the United States.

Jim was very proud to be an Olympic hero, but he also was respectful of his opponent. He stood and shook hands with the players from Japan, thanking them for the competition. Then he looked up and saw his teammates taking a victory lap around the field of the stadium. It was too late for

Team USA won the Olympic gold medal and Jim was the hero.

Jim to join them, but he didn't mind. He was happy to be thanking the Japanese. Besides, they soon returned to him for more hugs. One of Jim's teammates planted an American flag on the pitcher's mound. Jim laughed. All of the victories and awards he received could not compare to this moment.

"I'm sore all over," he said afterward. "But it was worth it. I'd do it 1,000 times over. I loved it."

A few days later, it was time for the awards ceremony. The stadium was full again, and viewers from around the world watched on television as Jim and his teammates stepped up on the platform and received their gold medals. It was the proudest day of Jim's life.

"This is my dream of a lifetime," Jim said.

There were many more dreams to come.

Chapter 6

Jim slipped his game jersey on over his head and tucked it in. He looked down at it, and there, in big red letters across the front, was the word ANGELS. Jim rubbed the letters with his fingers. He reached into his locker and took out his cap and put it on. He thought about how he hard he had worked to get this far. "Finally," he said, "I'm getting a chance."

Jim walked out to the spring training stadium field in Yuma, Arizona, and the cameras clicked furiously. He stepped up on the mound and began throwing his warm-up pitches. The stands were filled with fans who had come to see if Abbott had the stuff to pitch in the big leagues. Jim would be facing the San Diego Padres. The first batter stepped into the batter's box. Jim looked in for the sign from catcher Lance Parrish. Jim had always considered Lance a hero when he played for Jim's hometown Tigers several years earlier. Now, Jim and Lance were teammates. Lance called for a fastball. Jim reared back and delivered. The ball burst into Lance's glove for a strike. The radar gun timed it at 94 miles an hour. The crowd buzzed. Two more pitches, and Jim struck out the batter. Then he struck out the next batter. The final batter of the inning bounced out to first base.

The Angels had expected Jim to start the regular season in the minors—probably at double-A Midland, Texas. Few players skipped the minor leagues to go directly to the major league club, even first-round picks like Abbott. Jim was still just trying to get comfortable about pitching against the pros. "Just looking around at everything here," he said, "it hits you. A big-league camp."

Jim continued to impress the team with his mature attitude and his superb pitching. "He probably has as strong an arm as any left-hander I've ever caught," Parrish said. "His motion is so fluid, the ball just kind of explodes."

When the Angels' manager Doug Rader posted the team's roster for the major-league season, Jim's name was on it. There was no way the coaches could keep such a gifted young pitcher like Abbott off the team. Jim was named to the starting staff, and he would get his first assignment in a few days in Anaheim against the Seattle Mariners. Jim knew that just because he made the big-league team, it didn't mean he would be successful. Only nine pitchers since 1965 went directly from high school or college to the pro level without any minor-league experience—and none of them won more than six games their first year.

The large gathering of media surrounded Jim once again, this time at the Big A in Anaheim, where the Angels play their home games. Jim was about to pitch in his first major-league game—and he was extremely nervous. He had been in many big games before, but for some reason he couldn't stop the butterflies in his stomach this time. Maybe it was because he had dreamed of this day for so long. He was about to face Mark Langston, the ace of the Mariners' staff, who a year later would become Jim's teammate with the Angels.

Jim was excited to join the California Angels.

Jim strode out to the mound as he heard his name announced over the loudspeaker. The crowd cheered its appreciation for Abbott. The first batter, Harold Reynolds, singled to right field. Henry Cotto followed with another single, and both runners eventually scored to give Seattle a 2–0 lead. Abbott was too excited and too nervous to settle down. In the fifth inning, Rader had to come out to the mound to tell him he was through for the night. Jim was very disappointed because he knew he could do better. He gave up six runs on six hits and three walks. The Angels went on to lose, 7–0.

A horde of reporters surrounded Jim at his locker after the game, and Jim told them, "There was definitely some nervousness there. Maybe I wasn't as clearly focused as I should have been. I definitely didn't have my good stuff."

Five days later, Jim pitched again, this time against the mighty Oakland A's. He gave up a home run in the first inning to Dave Henderson, but then he settled down to shut out the A's for the next four innings. In the sixth, the A's started hitting. They scored three runs on Jim, and he was taken out of the game. The A's won 5–0. Jim felt better about this outing than the first one against the Mariners, but he wasn't satisfied. He knew he could win in the major leagues, and he wasn't about to give up. Neither were the Angels' coaches.

Eleven days later, against the Baltimore Orioles, Jim finally got some run support from his teammates. He took advantage of it by pitching six strong innings to win the game 3–2 for his first major-league victory. He allowed the Orioles just four hits and became the first Angel rookie left-hander to win a game in eight years.

A month later, he faced the Boston Red Sox and superstar pitcher Roger Clemens. Jim wasn't expected to win, but when

Jim became a starting pitcher right when he joined the Angels and he never pitched in the minors.

the Angels scored five runs in the first inning off Clemens, Jim knew he had a chance. He came through for his teammates by not allowing a run and pitching his first complete game. He allowed only three hits the entire nine innings. Later in the year, Jim shut out the Red Sox again for another victory. The word was out—Jim Abbott was no fluke.

Hitters around the league were beginning to fear Jim's fastball, which was traveling up to 95 miles an hour. Paul Molitor of the Milwaukee Brewers said, "If he can look past his disability the way he has, then my advice to batters who face him is that they better do the same thing."

In all, Jim won twelve games in his rookie season, twice as many as any pitcher to skip the minor leagues since the amateur draft began twenty-four years earlier. It was also the most wins by an Angel rookie in sixteen years.

The story of how Jim battled to overcome his disability spread across the country, and Jim became a hero to many people. He was featured in *Sports Illustrated, Newsweek, Time, People* magazine, and countless other publications, and he appeared on ESPN, CNN, "Good Morning America," the "Phil Donahue Show," and other television programs throughout the United States and around the world.

Jim would get hundreds of letters every week from fans—so many that the Angels had to keep his mail in shopping carts.

Through it all, Jim tried to stay focused on baseball. He answered as many letters as he could but he also had to make time for his career. He was only a rookie, still learning the ropes. He wanted people to remember that he was pitcher, not just a person who could play baseball with one hand.

Abbott won twelve games his rookie year and became an instant hero to many people.

Chapter 7

Jim listened to the radio talk show as caller after caller argued that he should be sent down to the minors. The callers complained that Abbott had no control. They said he needed to learn a slow curve or breaking ball to go with his power pitches. Jim read the newspapers and noticed that the columnists were writing the same thing.

It was true. Jim was having a terrible beginning to the 1991 season. He was 0–4 with a 6.00 earned-run average.

The criticism didn't bother Jim. In fact, he was glad to see it. Not once, in all the different complaints he was hearing or reading about, did anyone mention his disability. For the first time that Jim could remember, he was being judged simply as a pitcher. He always wanted to be thought of as just another player. It looked like that time had finally come.

As for the complaints, the Angels weren't about to send Abbott down to Triple A. Pitching coach Marcel Lachemann said that if the Angels sent Jim to the minors, they would have to send Marcel, too. Jim appreciated the support.

After a great rookie season, Jim had a difficult second

year. He was only 10–14 and allowed more hits than any other American League pitcher. But his record was a little deceiving. Jim didn't get very much run support from his teammates. In Jim's 14 losses, the Angels scored a total of 15 runs while he was in the game. A pitcher can't win too many games when his team scores just one run a game while he is pitching.

Now Jim was off to a tough start again in his third year, and people began to wonder if he really had the stuff to be a major-league pitcher. But instead of giving up on Abbott so easily, the Angels helped him improve. The coaches decided that Jim should forget trying to pitch with finesse as he had begun doing. They told him to just let it fly as hard as he could. That was how he had become so good in the first place. Jim admitted that he didn't feel relaxed on the mound, and the team psychologist taught Jim to talk to himself on the mound. This would get him to calm down. Teammate Luis Polonia even gave Jim his good-luck voodoo doll, and Jim put it in his locker.

All of this help brought results. Jim became better than ever before. He won his next four games, beating the Baltimore Orioles, Cleveland Indians, New York Yankees, and Chicago White Sox. In the four games, Jim allowed a total of six earned runs. All of a sudden, he was having fun out on the mound. "It's like it was in college," Jim told reporters. "I enjoy going out and pitching again."

Jim won five of his next nine games, and then he really caught fire. From early August into September, he pitched in seven games and won all seven to raise his record to 16–8. In that stretch, he gave up only 11 runs, which easily made him the most dominant pitcher in baseball. Jim's teammates always knew Jim could be a talented pro pitcher, but even they were surprised at how great he could be.

There was still plenty to learn about pitching in the majors.

"Several times I've seen him with legitimate no-hit kind of stuff, where nobody's even come close to attacking the ball," said third baseman Gary Gaetti.

The Angels were struggling as a team. They were in last place for over a month when Abbott took the mound at the Big A against the Brewers in early September. The Angels really wanted to get out of last place, but they were able to score only one run in the game. Jim knew he had to keep the Brewers from scoring for his team to win the game. He threw as hard as he could, and he talked to himself on the mound to stay "focused." Inning after inning, the Brewers swung and missed at Jim's rocket fastball. In the sixth, they managed to load the bases with two outs, but Jim got the next batter to hit into a harmless groundout to end the inning. He didn't allow a single run and had given up only five hits when a reliever came in for him in the seventh inning. Jim rooted from the dugout as the reliever saved the game. The Angels won the game 1–0, and they finally got out of last place.

A month later, on the second-to-last day of the season, it was Jim's turn to pitch again. This would be his final appearance of 1991, and he wanted to end the season with a victory. He faced the Kansas City Royals at the Big A, and nearly 30,000 people came out to see him. Cold air whipped through the stadium, but nobody seemed to mind as they watched Jim try to give the Angels another win. The Angels scored a run in the fourth inning and then Parrish, Jim's catcher and friend, hit a two-run homer to make it 3–0. The Royals were a hard-hitting team but Jim shut them down. He committed a balk in the sixth inning to give the Royals their only run. The Angels scored two more runs to make it 5–1 and Jim continued to throw strikes past the Royal hitters. As the last batter in the ninth inning stepped into the batter's box, the crowd rose to its feet, hoping for one final out: The batter

Jim became a star for the Angels after learning to stay "focused."

popped up, and the ball was caught by an infielder. The crowd exploded in a loud cheer for Jim, and he ran off the mound toward home plate to hug Parrish. It was a great season for Jim, especially since he had started so poorly. He finished with an 18–11 record and a 2.89 earned-run average, among the best in the American League.

Reporters and camera crews gathered around Jim in the locker room for the last time of 1991, asking what he thought of his finest major-league season. "I was able to put a lot of things into place this year that I learned from my first couple of years," Jim said. "I went through a lot of ups and downs my first two years and I had some ups and downs early this year, too. With the help of pitching coach Marcel Lachemann I was able to put it all into perspective, all the lessons."

Jim was still learning, but he really came far in 1991. Lachemann said, "Jimmy's just a good kid. He came along so quick. He just keeps trying to win and get better. He's probably one of the best in the league right now."

The media thought so, too. They picked Jim as the third-best pitcher in the American League in the Cy Young Award voting. He was pleased with the showing but even more proud of the way he turned his season around. He realized that he finally figured out how to be a great pitcher in the major leagues. Jim couldn't help thinking there were more great moments to come.

Chapter 8

The letters from fans come pouring into the Angels' office every day. They are addressed to "Jim Abbott-pitcher," and they tell how Jim has been such an inspiration. Jim gets over 100 letters every day. He reads every letter and tries to write back to as many people as he can.

Jim remembers when he first started playing baseball in the Greater Flint Youth Baseball Program. It's motto: "Every kid can play." That meant Jim could play. It didn't matter that he had only one hand. Jim wanted the other kids to treat him like a normal person, but they didn't always do that. They teased him. He knows there are a lot of other people out there who are going through the same sort of frustration. Jim always wanted to be just a major-league pitcher, but he knows that he has become much more than that. He is a hero.

One of the letters Jim received when he first joined the Angels was from an Indiana girl who had been mauled by a lion. Jim wrote back and said, "As your parents probably told you, I was born without my right hand. That automatically made me different from the other kids around. But know what? It made me different only in their eyes. I figured this is what the Good Lord wanted me to work with, so it was my responsibility to become as good as I could at whatever I chose to do, regardless of my handicap. I just won my first major-league game two days ago. At the final out, a lot of things went through my mind: My parents, all the help they provided; my brother and his support; all my frustrations along the way . . ."

One time when Jim was on the road with the Angels, a lady climbed onto the Angels' team bus and said to the first coach she saw, "Will you tell that kid with one arm that I have a little boy with a birth defect and what he's doing means a lot to us."

This sort of thing happens everywhere Jim goes. He is constantly asked how he overcame his disability. Jim always

Jim is always making friends with physically challenged kids.

explains that what he did was work with what he had. He never believed he was different from anyone else.

"I never felt I had to overcome anything," Jim explained in *Healthy Kids* magazine. "If I wanted to join my friends for a game in the park, I just did it. I don't ever remember waking up and saying to myself, 'Today, I'm going to go out and play baseball with one hand.' When I was little, my parents encouraged me to be outgoing and to not be afraid to face a challenge head-on. My dad was always telling me that when I'd see someone new I should walk up to them, shake their hand and say, 'Hi, my name is Jim Abbott.' My dad never wanted me to be held back because of my hand."

Ever since Jim has been in the public spotlight, first when he starred at Michigan, then when he pitched in the Olympics, and now when he is a major-league pitcher for the Angels, he has been interviewed by reporters and radio and television stations from all over the country and the world. They always ask the same questions over and over again. Jim has shown remarkable patience. He listens to the questions and then takes his time to answer them very clearly, even though he has heard them a thousand times before. Some of the questions are very insensitive. One time a reporter asked Jim if any other members of his family are "deformed." Jim handles these questions calmly because he knows how important it is for people to understand that he is really no different from anybody else. Still, it is very tiring to have to talk about the same thing all the time. Jim says it is harder than pitching. "The biggest challenge has been dealing with people and the media," he says.

Through it all, Jim is still just a young man learning to be a better pitcher. People seem to forget that. He has faced many challenges in the last few years, but it seems that he is the one who is giving all the support. Most young people with the

Above all, Jim has fun playing baseball with teammates like Gary Gaetti.

pressure of trying to be a big-time pitcher would need advice. Jim finds himself as the one giving the advice to others. No matter what the situation is, Jim remains positive.

"You have to have a positive attitude or you won't get anywhere," he says. "You can't be worried about failing because failure is a part of life—a very big part. You just have to keep on trying and pushing ahead and one day it will pay off. When an obstacle of any kind pops up in your life, don't sit down and give up. Maybe it sounds corny, but to me an obstacle is simply a step you have to climb over to achieve your goal. People who do that and aren't afraid to meet a challenge are the real heroes in my book."

Jim Abbott never gives up. No matter how difficult things may seem, he keeps on trying. He wants everyone else to do the same.

Career Statistics

Year	Team	W	L	ERA	G	GS	CG	IP	H	R	ER	BB	SO
1989	Angels	12	12	3.92	29	29	4	181.3	190	95	79	74	115
1990	Angels	10	14	4.51	33	33	4	211.6	246	116	106	72	105
1991	Angels	18	11	2.89	34	34	5	243.0	222	85	78	73	158
1992	Angels	7	15	2.77	29	29	7	211.0	208	73	65	68	130
1993	Yankees	11	14	4.37	32	32	4	214.0	221	115	104	73	95
Totals		58	66	3.66	157	157	24	1061	1087	484	432	360	603

Where to Write Jim Abbott:

Mr. Jim Abbott
c/o California Angels
Anaheim Stadium
Anaheim, CA 92806

Index